•

Lumen, Inc.
40 Camino Cielo
Santa Fe, New Mexico 87506
lumenbooks.org

Distribution:
Consortium Book Sales
800 283-3572
www.cbsd.com

Cover painting:
First Bed Painting, 1988
Jesper Christiansen

•

A Bedroom Occupation
Love Elegies

Mark Scott

Foreword

Richard Howard

The subtitle, "Love Elegies," and the very *look* on the page of this carefully titrated series of two dozen amorous programs (somewhere between the seductive and the sermonical, their diction demotic, their temper short, their costume loose-fitting and ready for action) is a directive clue: we are in Horatian country, a disabused (because *already abused*) region of discourse extending from Tibullus and Propertius to Ovid and Juvenal. But though his first book of poems, *Tactile Values*, was redolent with discreet behaviors and quizzical sagesse, young Mark Scott pays no *respects* to the Roman erotic elegy so tellingly to be noted in his second: who ever overheard glossy Horace adjuring himself, as this argument runs, "How out in front of it can you be? That's the real question. You can forget your conflict / avoidance and your business models. / That's all academic. This is real-world we're talking, boots on the ground. . . . Save the lecture." The words exchanged are bywords and passwords, anything but polite, though often bitterly *juste*: "Mars / has canals, they say. Well so the fuck does Venice, / and look at the Venetians. They're drowning, sinking, getting muddy. The whole world / is mud." And these exchanges occur between a company of out-for-sex buddies and fair-weather girlfriends (Cynthia indeed, speaking of Propertius, and who in hell is Paul?) with occasional outtakes by Dickinson and Swift. *Drôle de monde*. But what can you call a world where the only knowledge is cracked or crooked, the only ignorance vulnerable or virulent? I call it comical, all right, even cynical, but the most heart-breaking love poetry since that other Empire fell.

CONTENTS

A Bedroom Occupation
Love Elegies

In going to my naked bed as one that would have slept . . .

—Richard Edwardes, 1523-1566

I

Lewis, you tell me not to choose my freedom, a desolate heart, but to remain in delight
       with one woman. Too late; I moved out; I can't retrieve
that message where you sent it: Lauren changed our code. And if I could, why should
       what works for our friend work for me? He seems happy,
says he's comfortable (which reminds him he doesn't have "the fuck-you money yet").
       And he's consistent, stable. But his waters don't run deep.
Mine do—or so I've been told. "If that's how you feel," Lauren said, "you'd better
       move out." At my new address, the first thing I did was vacate.
It looked like a loading dock at UPS: empty boxes—but not of California wine, Florida
       lemons, grapefruits from Texas. Like Emerson in one of his
moods, I got only the discontent of what I wanted, books, the desolation you spoke of.
       No sooner had I shelved them than I found myself,
short of cash, hawking some for a song on Telegraph. Which reminds me: you know how
       I always said I wished I could find again the voice that was great
within that night in Boulder, when I got hold of "Wild Night," on bourbon and LSD?
       (No wonder our troubadours died young.) Well, I'm taking
voice lessons. If my career as a bodyworker is any guide, my singing life will expire
       in ninety days, too, but I'll get it while I can. You were
right, though, about my preoccupation: delightlessly I've slept with four women
       since moving in, and the fifth I paid for.

II

What hardened me years ago, Cynthia, wasn't the sparse hair on your cunt, but your
       calf under the table, in Bob's kitchen; that was the prime
mover. My mother's age you are, give or take, but nothing like my mother: you'd spend
       a decade composing a fugue for Woodrow Wilson,
but she never would. You weren't my mother—I see it now—but my aunt, my mother's
       little sister, who still, at fifty, kept her long hair in a French
braid, and kept the air of riding horseback through a world that had turned on her,
       like your husbands, before she'd had time to age.
To age! To grow up is hardly the same. Youth lies to age. I lied the night you cooked me
       dinner—but I sniffed out the green weed on your breath,
the martini you drank to turn down your nerves for my arrival. You chopped onions;
       I, thirty years off your life, gazing into photograph:
your daughter, standing beside you on a beach, kite string in hand; the sand in your sandy
       hair, the sun, the wind. You chopped tomatoes, cucumbers,
parsley; I flipped through your records: *The Moonlight Sonata*, the *Appassionata*.
       "You've never heard the *Appassionata*? A virgin!"
I should have demurred. Dinner burned as we touched, the tone gone from the muscles
       in your thighs, the suppleness gone from your breasts,
but your calves! Hogarth's line of beauty, my palms, your tears, fit. I kissed your closed
       eyes, your cheeks, that smile on your lips, older than the rocks.
I'd heard the *Appassionata* before, but only last summer. The young woman who'd put it
       on, a diver, ten years younger than you are on that beach,
than I on your hips, took me out into the moonlight, *allegro assai* (she was full of plans),
       and we made love as Beethoven spun.

III

Mark, why do you shoot so many young women when you have a perfectly good wife
       at home? True, you never see her. She works, you work.
You should never have married in the first place; everyone at the wedding harbored
       that thought, even your mother. You went through with it
for her, I suspect, and for the neighbors we grew up with, whose names you can never
       remember. But the young women in frames around
my studio, prints you've signed: why haven't we shared the particles of our lusts
       for them? We don't know if we differ here,
as in so many other respects. You know that I can name both names of all my lovers
       seriatim, going back twenty years (we're forty now,
like Casanova in volumes 7 & 8). This pleased you, as most acts of remembrance do.
       But let me tell you what would please me:
photographs, of course, of Paula's mouth (that mouth of mouths, everywhere repeating)
       kissing mine, of Heidi's thighs, of Lauren in the snow
by the creek where the ouzels dip, of Missy's lap in the barn. You stop these things
       in time, pose, light, and charm them into that
chemical bath; I envy what can't be captured. So don't be flattered: from the start,
       women exerted themselves in and on your behalf.
I spoke this summer with Anna, Susan, and Kathy: they've almost forgotten
       the impression of your bed; still, I'm sure
you're safe. Should they chance to read this, they'll get no closer to your secret than they
       got to you. (The roll that's been exposed can't be
developed.) Haven't I gotten closest? Remember that poster above your bed,
       of the early Lauren Hutton? What was it you said about
the gap between her teeth, or the gap between her thighs? "The look is everything."
       But even then, everything wasn't enough.

IV

She's gone, Lewis, the woman who's looking for Mr. Right Now. "Now" can now be
        measured: we met at eight for coffee, she dressed
and drove away at midnight. It might have been noon, for all I knew. I smoked
        an American Spirit and walked to the corner,
to see if the streetwalkers were out. Not that I would have asked; I was satisfied, it was
        late. The one who drove away was sixty.
"Dependable & intimate friendship," her personal read, but the message when I called
        began with a dependent clause: "Although
I'm mainly looking for a sexual partner . . ." She didn't miss a beat when, finished with
        dinner, we got to "the sticky part." Pure Teflon:
I said I'd straightened up my studio, she said she'd cleaned house. On her futon fifteen
        minutes later, I asked after the safety of my mouth,
which she gave clearance to. And would she like me to? She would, I did.
        "That was fun." I'm losing all proportion
in my love, Lewis—if, unlike most poets, I take the popular latitude with that word,
        miserable monosyllable. You won't wonder
what possessed her, a full-blown dahlia, but what me? And the Angelas of last semester,
        one and twenty, *ubi sunt*? No use to talk to me.
Suppose we did it for the material it would afford (she writes stories), to which I
        make you witness now. An unintended image,
Donne-like, of her age, caught me in her ad: "ash-blonde hair." That's all that's left.
        Youth and age produce the same smooth
hands that feel, lips that take in. And one more thing: she's learning, she said, to ask
        for what she wants; but in the meantime, this
"ash-blonde beauty" will take what she gets—a "talkative and quiet" thirty-eight-year-old,
        infrequent, not intimate.

V

Janet raised her arms toward the ceiling and nodded. I wrapped the sheet around her
        and clenched it behind. She lay down on the table,
supine, then hiked herself over on her side. My task was a longitudinal release
        on her erector spinae, finishing on her latissimus.
In preparation, I warmed her skin with the flat of my hand, then rolled the scale of her
        rib cage. Her upper-back was small, the small smaller.
Cervical, thoracic, lumbar: I rolled my way down. Her eyes closed once or twice;
        she praised my touch. I couldn't return
the compliment. "You have warm hands," I managed, still feeling them from an hour
        before, during her turn. Under the *Deep Forest* music
that played, Janet spoke. No other students could hear, though what she said was meant
        for them, for slighting her: "You can kiss my ass."
I froze, Lewis, then took my bearings: my hands were on her greater trochanter,
        my mouth a foot from that. Had she said
"my gluteus maximus," or "my gluteus minimus" (a harder place for the lips to reach),
        or even "my anus," the class had surely heard her.
As a rule, it's the vernacular, with its dead figures, that cheapens us, not the learned.
        But here, in the *sotto voce* of a defiant born-
again, slang restored us, made us priceless. Life, friends, is serious; and for the first
        time in mine, I could take someone literally.
Five minutes back, I too had hated Janet. She alone had kept the seventh game from us.
        But that had been the rule we'd agreed on
when we enrolled: *Deep Forest* only while we worked, unless unanimous we
        voted otherwise. Looking down on her now
as she lay naked on her side, a sheet of cotton blend her only cover, I asked
        if she was all right, knowing she wasn't.

I sided with her; I admired her. And what more pleasurable than the feel of admiration?

I noticed her eyes for the first time.

Lebanese? Portuguese? Beautiful, hurt eyes. Inserting a pillow for comfort between her

knees, I saw her calves. I wanted to petrissage them,

her strong gastrocnemius, the soleus beneath her skin. But the task was a longitudinal

release on the spinae, the muscle we erect ourselves with.

She adjusted a pillow beneath her head, then asked for another, which she placed

in defense of her breasts. As she did, the sheet slipped,

and I saw one of the two things, both cleavages, that I was not supposed to see. The room

was quiet. The fetal position had infantilized

half the people in it. I started my slack, sink, and move manipulations on the most medial

part of the erector, the spinalis. Janet's was ropey.

I tried to soften it by separating its fibers in the fascia, that lubricious tissue, the anterior

inner surface of the skin—the skin's skin. It slid

and rolled beneath my hands like a puppy's. My penis, which had been getting heavier,

now hardened to the inferior, exceeding the quadriceps

hem of my boxers, its cold, dry face to show. Fortunately, Janet was turned away.

"Let's take some deep breaths," I said.

Overcompensating on her spine, my reinforced thumb bounced off either her illiocostalis

or her longissimus, and I found myself doing two things

a bodyworker should never do: think, and lose contact. Now I had my hands full.

An erection's Platonically proprioceptive:

it experiences itself in space immediately, but has no idea where it's going—only

the urge for going. My hands left Janet's frame

to move my stiffened member in a more medial and posterior direction, but I stopped

in mid-motion: I had to reestablish contact.

Back in the lumbar region, above the iliac crest and nearing the quadratus lumborum,

        I saw the superior hem of Janet's underpants.

Was she in her period, too, like my client of two days before, or simply modest?

        Not normally receptive to the blandishments of lace,

I had to admit—or my erection did—that today was not normal. In an advice column

        I'd read that morning (I read two a week),

the advisor, a woman, diagnosed her correspondent's problem with a shocking

        conventionality: she wasn't getting any.

Janet's fundamental Christianity, her strange choice of vocation, her bald utterance,

        her breast pillow, her lace panties—perhaps

they all added up: not only wasn't Janet getting any, but Janet had never gotten any.

        And now, as I was in a position to give her some,

so she was to receive. Lewis, I backed away—away from lumborum toward latissimus

        dorsi, rhomboid, and trapezius, that bumper-to-bumper

interchange on the freeway of stress. I asked her once again to breathe. What would I do?

        A passive stretch, but there was nothing to push against,

and the Greek tragedy of the musculature, agonist and antagonist, was not yet

        sufficiently known to me. I couldn't recall

what I did know. Distracted by my own flesh and blood, I was merely pushing

        skin. Adjusting my lunge, I bore down

to petrissage her lumborum, deep to the latissimus. She winced; I lost touch

        again. As I rejoined her, a sympathetic spasm

pinched my own lumborum and, pain being for me a great deflector of desire,

        flaccid I finished the release.

VI

I couldn't live with you, Doug; I can't imagine how Kathy can, and I love you as much as
  she, as a man can who doesn't sleep with men.
We've done the things our kind of man's supposed to do: cycled hills, played catch
  with several kinds of ball, talked of balling, drunk beer,
smoked dope, chewed tobacco. Kathy's never with us when we do our duty to the state
  of man. What does she do, think, say, once we've
had our way? I hope it's something greater than the proper study of mankind. She likes
  to cook; she loves to play piano, keep your books (one set).
Her looks leave nothing to be desired—which is every man's excuse to stray, and we've
  talked often of straying. Let's face it: we've strayed.
So what keeps you two together? My break was short, mercifully; I had thought yours
  shorter, but Kathy answered when I called just now.
I can tell you this, there in Andalucia, or Madrid, or Sevilla: the rain stays mainly
  on the plain, and it will be the same at home
as when you left it. In twenty years, when we're sixty, "we'll be alone" (I quote you).
  Perhaps you need a month to spin your wheels;
then you'll accept it. But what do I know? I'm a faithless man, trying still to win the race
  or game I was never really in when I was twenty-one,
or ten. That age, according to my father, determined the state I'm in: aroused by danger,
  doused with grief, by grief aroused, all danger doused.
At least you have a house and a business. I have doubt to fall back on, but doubt that
  doubt will break my fall, if I fall; you doubt that any man can.

VII

I would take and blazon you part by part across this page, if I could, looking back, feeling
        back, remember parts of you alone, apart from
how they differed from parts of Sara, parts of Kay, parts of a hundred others. But I'm
        neither Petrarch nor Sidney, Cavalcanti nor Villon;
and I decline to amalgamate or idealize. Your left breast, Kate, must have its mole,
        your aureoles their hair, their jagged crests
like cirques in Switzerland or Mono Lake; your abs, tight as tape around the cap
        of a vitamin bottle. What else? The pregnant
hinges of your knee, as if you'd given birth from there to something genuine, like you.
        Zeus or Semele carried Dionysus in thigh;
you pouched yourself for delivery, twenty-four years after your birth, in Taos. Notice:
        I skipped your head, where all true blazons start,
because your hair persists in changing color. I never stroke the same shade twice.
        Your eyes: last week when you were here
I could have told you they were green and clean, unworldly; today, I'm not so sure—
        hints of brown, highlights of rust?
I'm warning you: you love me too much; too freely you spirit your body around,
        fucking me like that. A scandal of energy,
you dance in the desert now, sending back in Buddhist epistles and Welsh metaphors
        your reasonable fears of abandonment.
But it's you, Kate, in a script almost Ottoman, who keeps wanting to call me "baby,"
        and keeps promising, under separate cover, a cactus.

VIII

Cynthia, I'm sick, and you wouldn't believe how it's altered my libido for the worse.
       My will's not even intact. What can you promise
to make me feel better? What would you offer if I came? Thinking through the things
       we did, the positions we took—we were very tame.
Mozart took more chances in a phrase from an early symphony than we took in two
       years of intercourse and correspondence. Just talking
to you, though, makes me feel better, as my mother used to say. She was fond of feeling
       better, being cheerful, which always pained me.
I would leave if I could, and seek some anaesthetic. Remember when we sat opposed
       on the hardwood floor upstairs, after a bath?
Tantric, I think you said it was, the waiting; but I had to travel to come. You were always
       disappointed in me—my youth, my impatience,
my sitting on your chest with nothing interesting to say. This little cold I'm having
       reminds me of your jaded, sleepy partnership.
I disappointed my first lover, as if she'd said to me, "You look so small, not a king
       at all." I was thirteen, fourteen. Christ!
I thought the expectation was all mine; so should have been the feelings attending
       the failure to meet it. Here they come now,
like friends who are never on time. (That germ of resentment.) I saw an add for seed
       of all ethnicities in the free weekly today,
followed closely by those lines from *Thick as a Brick*: "your sperm's in the gutter,
       your love's in the sink." Onan the Barbarian!
Urge on urge, all things rush upstream, heart-ward like the bodyworker's
       strokes, wearing their spawning colors out.

IX

It's dark, you're tired, your little cold persists, and you're alone. Aren't we supposed to
       generate companions from within, without
attachments, from secret sins, and live happily never after? Defaced, abstract, metallic
       talk seems all your harvest, a grim sum
scarcely nourishing. Your keyboard for a fuck! Fifty dollars you made for a "program"
       on "Where Poems Come From"
for the Browning Society "girls," and you would spend it on pussy in the street,
       if you had it still; but one must eat.
The wet flesh, the surviving lubricity: empty cup, then full tea. Tit: Tintoretto, that
       elephantine infant, imagines the Milky Way
as from the nipple gushing—as Beth's breasts leak when you gum to her whisper,
       "Suck harder, you can go harder." Difficult
to take in, vaguely bitter, thick briefly, then thin. Your mother never nursed you,
       but she does, without conception or term,
her ancient pregnant figure trading with you pre-come for pre-come. No woman's
       made you run with such anticipation
at that fish-like mouth down there, eyelet of a pole. She likes to watch you please
       yourself, to strain against your hold
while she pulls back her hair and ties it off, eyes calm and wide (because you peek
       you know). Prone you roll,
for her to fuck you, ill-equipped as she is. She tastes instead, and with her tongue abides:
       you press the mattress in fear,
then take a turn until your jaw gets sore. Mum, you let her thighs stop your ears.

X

Only one thing in my life I planned, Lewis, one goal: this—and to be in bed alone
        when I want at night, and not when I don't.
As I talk in my sleep, canting the best things to no one, most of my life achieves
        most of my goal. When companioned,
neither I nor the one who shares my bed thinks enough of what I utter to rise and write it
        down, and I fall short (and back to sleep).
I rarely know what talk my sleep is soothed or lightened by, and so when not alone,
        I have to be reminded, but not verbatim,
which brings me no solace, as you might imagine—to lose those effortless good things,
        words that might have made more of this casuistry
than my waking mind (such as it is) can. Alone is best, then. With Lauren, though,
        I could both compose myself and sleep,
after eight years, undisturbed by an intimacy presumed, a masquerade in the dark,
        by embarrassed attempts to revive what was at best
memorial, at worst moribund—this wretched sex, or whatever we call it,
        we make so much of. Was it Schwartz
or Crane who said, "In this town, poetry's a bedroom occupation"? Akron, Oakland,
        Snowmass, Manhattan—in what town isn't it?

XI

Paul, you bored, indifferent lover, Doug's been keeping me abreast of the dangers
        you court and the baldness you face.
You're the fourth man I can think of (I'm the third) whose most eminent feature
        is resignation. We should have been impeached,
for all we got away with, and still do, but the political will is lacking. Wanting to do
        the right thing—we were raised with manners—
we at least partially penalize ourselves with a work-force slow-down, striking
        with an impassivity impressive to those
who fire away on all cylinders and never sleep (one of whom called the other night,
        raving about Céline, whose un-air-conditioned nightmares
I'm not familiar with). What's with us, Paul? You go to visit your father's grave,
        who came to one of your games. Your strikes
that night were balls, your balls strikes; but it wasn't enough that the opposing team
        cleaned your clock: the old man had to
get in his innings. You surprised yourself when he died by kneeling on his sunken
        mound. But that was nothing to the sequel,
when your back locked and you had to crawl back to the car. Your mother's name's
        Gloria: need I say more? If we were books,
our titles would be *Sick Transit* and *Finishing Touch*. Had we been born before
        the tables turned, when doubtless Touch
held its own at the bottom of the standings, and Sight was no bush-league scout,
        we would have played by those rules.
We love rules. It's statistics that numb us, the percentages they're always going with.
        Those five years of college, those were the days!
You fucked them all, on the up and up, consensually, and I admired your range.
        Charm you had in spades, but carelessly,

as the slick song says: "Hold on loosely." Doug tells me women still tail you

     in supermarkets, and men,

when they see you coming, stop their hunting, turn tail, drive away.

XII

So you're moving in, Celeste, as I move on, setting up house for two as I set up,
        with four used Thonet chairs (already "classic"
in the magazines), for one. Didn't Woolf say that nothing is ever one thing? The Buddhist
        dispensing a voice too crafted and cool
in the *Bateau Ivre* wants something "more interesting," and so do I, though I'd never
        put it that way. But perfectly intelligent people
couch their desires (you bought a new couch?) in the worn upholstery of that epithet.
        You say you want my "good mind"
there with you and Anna and Maggie in Maine; I want your good voice here in Oakland,
        where I've almost completed my collection
of Isaiah Berlin, and where my latest friend encourages me to be "spontaneous."
        She'll get no argument, not when this fox
is "in the mood," as she, who grew up on Cole Porter, and knows what he means, put it.
        As I was trying to say, no person is ever
one person, lives alone; but then again my grandmother, forlorn in the nursing home now,
        and many others, do live alone. I hope to
in my time—but without the "support network" that you, who hates surprises and stock
        phrases but welcomes deviltry in the afternoon,
surprise me by naming—and happily. Meanwhile, you know no one in Portland,
        I no one in Oakland, except those we do.
Today, I rely on you and Propertius, on seltzer and Alka-Seltzer Plus, on what this minute
        brings: nothing could be finer. But then you
register my depressing sound again. What shall I do with this voice? It belies me,
        that strangely self-reliant verb I here abuse.

XIII

The heavens didn't open, the waters didn't part, nor Pan shake the earth, Lewis;
        not this time. And in the aftermath of this non-event,
I report misgivings of another physical year. Why can't love intercalate a single week
        that hasn't been lived already, many times over?
Why should my regrets be taken as openings? Why should Kate insist that the insoluble
        problem of art and life swearing each other off
be spared the rest of us for her to solve? She admitted that the world may not have gotten
        up in her face yet; so I offered her an inventor's
creed: that impossible things only are worth working on. But love's neither impossible
        nor work. One knows what hits one.
When Leslie opened the door in Chicago, I knew. There had been love at first write;
        but writing, as you know, serves any able hand,
and ours happen to be. And so we proposed: "Why not meet off-line, in a neutral place,
        and see if we can't follow through, can't
take this further?" Couldn't. All we did was fuck for three nights quietly, skipping
        mornings and two afternoons—which pleased us,
was fun, felt good, worked; but it wasn't enough to interrupt our lives with.
        So she drove up north, I flew back west,
both to small towns. The squat city itself played an insignificant role, as did our
        presences, which did not passion. You and I
have read that they can, in such affairs; ours failed to. I thought you should know.
        And know I knew the outcome before the event.

XIV

You, Mark, or Peter Pan, when will you cease, at mere mention of a woman's name,
        to dart to what she might be, or think? How many

disappointments will satisfy you? How many moves? Your giant goes with you
        wherever you go, the Sage said, but what

did he know? One house, one place, one Concord all his life, and every day a walk
        at the same hour. Routine like that

would stifle you, wouldn't it? Jennifer shoved in today with Kate, Kàti, and Brenda,
        with Susan and the rest (there is no rest),

saying, "Maybe it's you boring and stifling yourself; maybe the riskless life you've been
        leading, the uncommitted playboy's selfish tour

you've been taking, is taking its toll on you; maybe saying an entire yes to someone else
        is what you need to do." Sounds like retreat,

at first blush, retreat from *persistive constancy*, as Shakespeare drew it, perseverance,
        with accent on the second syllable, as who

should say, *sever, severe*; or from that killing passage in "Self-Reliance," about whim,
        that came home to you in your black Vision

on the highway, near Ely, Peckinpah's retreat from Hollywood, through the six-speaker
        warmth of Dylan singing, "She's an artist,

she don't look back"—the charm of his misogyny, which you seem to have the knack of
        and fear, lately, being accused of. People

admire liberty, or intelligence, until you use it on them. And the retreat would be into
        what? Formulae, being understood.

But who doesn't like to say things that *almost but don't quite formulate*? Nobody doesn't,
        now and then. But as a career move?

O, reform it altogether! Near is the last breath the yellowing so suddenly succeeds.

XV

Cynthia says I'm nice, Lewis, and always have been. She asks if I want to drift
       the rest of my life. If not, she says, the thing
to do is "limit the sets of questions" by limiting the number of highly intelligent
       women I get involved with,
all of whom have questions to put—different questions, and hard. Be with one,
       she says, and you only have one set of questions.
"When that woman asks a question you can't answer, have a baby. That'll set everyone
       back about three years. Once you catch up,
you'll probably get another question put to you that you don't like or can't answer.
       Have another baby."
Why drag another person into it? But I do. I've counted the women I've loved,
       flirted with, written poems for, never touched,
become friends with, fucked. I have three incomplete lists. I doubt one of those women
       has a similar set. I don't doubt a few of them
think of me, as I of them, when a Cars or a Crosby, Stills, Nash, and Young song plays,
       or turtle oil or patchouli does to
"personal space" what an opened orange does to a room. I struggle with detachment,
       force myself not to think or speak
of attachment, but Cynthia sees through it; they all do. Freud said he had to be a little
       unwell to write well; I have to be a little detached
to be attached—being the one, usually, who loves less. I want sympathy for that.
       The more loving one gets it all
when the couple breaks up; otherwise, there's none for either party (most people
       secretly dislike lovers). I said no to Kate,
who wanted to get married and have children. Cynthia says I made a mistake, because
       Kate's the perfect age to have children.

I told her children wouldn't have come for three years. "You've been wasted," she said.

        "Why don't you just come to Princeton

and live with me in my new apartment? I'll keep you until you're ready (don't tell anyone

        where you are) and then I'll write you

a letter of recommendation." I laughed too, Lewis. The designs of the undesigning

        are the most intricate, especially

when the designers have money, and Cynthia does. "The only way through the impasse

        is to give yourself up," she added,

eliding "to me." "Everything you feel isn't right—unless you want to be a serial

        monogamist all your life." I'm not, I told her,

sometimes I have three or four lovers at the same time. She cut me for that. "I remember

        when you'd come to me. I used to think—

no, I used to feel terror in my heart: here comes the Great Emptiness. I'd rather

        have a glass of milk and watch TV

than listen to you. But your voice was always so gentle . . ."

XVI

Perhaps I should accuse you, Kate, of whoring. Like most men, I'd be false if I did.
>When men feel jealous of a woman,

they think she must be sleeping around; when she sleeps around, they don't even notice.
>Men are fools, as you know, and you seem to

like them that way. Of the two you're seeing now, the two I know of, one, you say,
>is like me—irresponsible, noncommittal, sensual;

the other, ready to marry you, have children with you, is, even in his designs on life,
>a Buddhist with a high-paying, steady job.

Him you refuse; the other, like me, is older; unlike me, he's your father's age. Berating
>me on the patio, over which the icicles melt

in the morning sun, and the snow, heaped here and there, muddies with the runoff,
>you suppose your early life with your father,

a philosopher manqué, confuses whatever the issue is you're trying to settle;
>I said as much five years ago, didn't I?

All is present tense; passion streams in the firmament the pines are pointing to;
>and I make the point you're tired of hearing,

a distinction between the disappointment you still feel at my not having asked
>for your hand in marriage—what you called

"being a man"—and the responsibility I took in refusing it; knowing, after knowing
>otherwise, that that was, for the worse then,

for the best now, as even then. Now, when chance is yours, where's your assent
>to what you wanted? The bird is in the hand,

Kate, but you keep your palm open. Timing wrong? Chemistry lacking? If this man now
>is not your man, I am not, nor was then.

XVII

Jocelyn, your top lip was sticking to your teeth today when you came by the office;
>   your lipstick was much too red.
Your hair thins daily; you should stop trying to look half your age: it ages you
>   beyond your beauty, that pale, infirm,
Swedish beauty two towns in the valley universally acknowledge. I know you're wary
>   of being looked upon, but all some people know
is your pretty face—not how capable you are, what a loner, what a poor manager of men
>   you make; not your enduring skin
I want to touch with, sometimes inflamed, excited and red, but unevenly (not as in
>   the "full-bleed scenic" brochure you
mocked-up for the fundraising committee). Your health has gone to your head, I think—
>   all that garlic, orange juice, olive oil and ginger
you blend each morning and take in ravenous little sips (if sips can be ravenous).
>   And the wrinkles, too, the feet around the eyes,
the skin drawing closer to the bone, a shadow of bruise on the bicep where the skin's
>   drying—resilience losing ground. Perhaps
it's an unintended effect of that concoction, to which your lip adheres when you would
>   smile or speak, spreading discomfort.
"Jocelyn isn't a team player," the veteran said of you today, prefacing her nod
>   to a candidate for your old job.
No one in the pit knows of our having teamed up, in bucket seats, across the emergency
>   brake, and then again, once, in a bed not quite
queen—yours. How well our wishes went then, once you darkened the room. A brake
>   checks our momentum, too: in anything
designed to move, a device to stop it. But you never let yourself go; you rode clutch
>   and brake as if motion sickened you;

spoke often of changing your life ("you writers have ruined me for other men"), but stuck

    to your routines. (As I did.) What could I say?

I side with the medical establishment, reach for aspirin, swallow remedies at sterile

    removes from what's organic.

"Love," one writer says, "isn't an illusion: it doesn't exist"; another, that it's what's

    left over after skepticism's applied to feeling.

I say, for now, it was your ass one day, in those pale blue jeans, when you happened

    and I happened to be turned

one way, from which whatever we've had swayed and still sways.

XVIII

You call me late at night, Kàti, demanding my attention, calling me "unstable in feeling."
        But you remain hopeful, funny
in your search for someone to adore, someone you can fold to or bend toward, for what's
        missing in you. Found, this would be love,
by your lights; but tonight, again, it or he is nowhere. Not behind the toilet, not under
        your dresser, not in your closet, not
sitting at your Nepalese temple to pray. Your bed, as I recall, is already on the floor—
        no sense looking under it. Romance,
on the other hand, I ask you to define: not malicious, you say, or demanding, it's play
        of the kind you're putting on with a man
now, a hundred miles away; a man who, if you saw him any more than you do, you say
        you wouldn't be seeing. Romance
is hard to find. You think you scared me off that time we tried to let it "access us,"
        lying on your futon side by side,
with a weak impression: neediness and instability—but yours, I'm afraid, not mine.
        And so by no intentions we're aware of,
we've wandered into affection of a kind your definition does and doesn't subsume:
        intermittent, tentative, abruptly generous,
the promise of surprise and deficit, brought on, you say, by my risk-averse device of
        seeming available, but to no avail,
stumped by the follow-through the form requires.

XIX

Say I am, Susan, trying to see if I can do without you. Say I am. "If you love me,"
       the German poet wrote, "what is that to me?"
Such things should be thought, but not set down, out of respect for all that could be
       forgotten; namely, sedater versions of love,
love less its countervailing force. All of Latin's been forgotten but the one conjugation:
       amo, amas, amat, and so on
through the *they*—as in, "They love each other," which is supposed to explain everything.
       You never loved your husband; to him,
you were cook and driver, manservant, little sister. His hobby and his income made do.
       My mother, she put something Talleyrand said
on her refrigerator: "What greater pleasure than dinner: it comes every day, and lasts
       an hour." True enough, but Talleyrand
never cooked a meal or washed a dish, two things at least my mother did for forty years:
       how quickly she forgets, making do
with that sacred hour, miracle of loaves and fish! You want to know where our lives
       "intersect," and I recall my mother.
Between us in age you come, Susan, between us in temper and scope. You say you know
       "there's no place for our relationship
to go"—no children, no . . . but what do I know? Unhappiness, you think, is my *métier*;
       the cooking and the dishes I think of,
not the hour squeezed out between, not the pleasure, not the fun, in order to do what I do,
       which gives you pause. And yet
your rogues' gallery, whose repugnant images you just reviewed (for timing, if
       nothing else) and replaced in the trunk,
by elimination yields me as the most likely. To which I say, "Why not?" and you laugh.
       Then we both think, "What for?"

XX

So you would know where poems come from, Susan? I can't answer that. But if you ask
        the source of mine, I can. Not confusion,
first of all, not beauty of the first degree, not emotion recollected in tranquility; not
        other poems and their poets; not
animus against another coming toward me, howsoever the travel is taken; not by way of
        vision, nor by a vision; not by hope or wish,
not in longing; neither through an image that encloses some complex in an instant,
        nor through vortices; not out of a spout
conjoining sea and sky, nor in a fable handed down by a tractatrice who washed and set
        the hair of peripatetic Greece
and marching Rome, that frantic seat, where Janus, looking before and after, could keep
        no peace; nor by strength of fields,
snatches of song or scent, last breath, ash; not out of envelopes that hold affairs in grief;
        nor from joy at relief or possible despair;
still less from the red-winged blackbirds' dart of scarlet, orange; from saying
        saxifrage and *persiflage*, from cumquat leaves
and blueberry, their waxen surface, gaugeless veins, that fruit bitter, this sweet,
        stem-end and *blossom-end,* plum-seam and peach-fold.

XXI

"Fuck the pussy," she said, when I was well in, "Get your nut." We weren't naked

       or in sheets. She made sure of the one,

I of the other. Our pants were just below our knees; she, propped against the foot

       of the bed. "It takes me time," I said proudly,

not wanting to be rushed. "Better not," she said, "I'm on the clock." Have you ever been

       spoken to like that, Lewis?

It took me back. Then, "You have a lot of books. You read novels? Who's your favorite

       author?" I can never answer that.

But here, it was as if I were in a recitation room and getting "screwed." (At Harvard,

       Emerson was content to be screwed—

if he could "accurately paint the fact" later, in his journal.) So I scanned my shelves

       for a candidate. "Dickens."

(I can hear you laugh.) "What's he write about? Sidney Sheldon's mine." The word

       "Victorian" was coming; I came instead.

"Good now," she said, pulling up her pants. "I told you I got good pussy."

       "You got another five dollars

in here, don't you?" I looked, but came up short. She'd shorted me, too, delivering

       only half the "half and half"

she'd promised; so I gave her my supply of condoms—three, to be exact—and some

       quarters I'd saved for the laundry.

XXII

I tell you Marbot consummated incest with his mother; you say, "Every boy's dream."
  But we're consummate, and you never recalled
my mother. Maybe incest with your son, who's just broken up with his girlfriend, is just
  the thing you need; maybe I should
explore it with my mom. I've fucked everything else I could lay my vain hands on,
  essaying once a neighbor's dog
and then its owner, as she reached up high in her closet at my factitious request. A horse
  would be the *dernier cri*
or *fois* (if I have the French right): to fuck the head of that complete creature, when all
  I've ever wanted is to cradle it
and wrestle it down, as a cowboy does a steer. For what? For love, all for love. But we've
  had this discussion, Sophia: how the man,
unable to bear beauty, has to want to bring it to a sprawl—exposed, contorted, complex—
  on the ground of whatever he thinks
his being is—flakes of kosher salt, the outskirts of town (*town*: quaint). For two years
  your occasions have all been barren,
and sixty presses in its approach. Dreams come, but, like old husbands, rarely come
  again; nor does your wanting help them to.
Desire's the rub—for the million fugitive and cloistered Burmese, many of them women;
  for Bellow, Kunitz, Cleopatra, and Shakespeare's
Achilles. Reasons more potent and heroic than our three-foot privacies prevail:
  'tis known we're in love, and what of it?
Something gives and something breaks. I break back, hale and deviant, embedded,
  erect in Plato's cave, my wrists
and neck hyper-extended. And I cry out, and you cry out, "Fuck me, fuck me."

XXIII

My breasts, Amy, licked softly, respond along a meridian that reaches my toes. All of me
       contracts. I wouldn't have guessed

I could be reached there, much less so completely. Disarmed, I even start to make sounds
       in bed, guttural and infantile, as if I were

on my side, knees bent—but what is that to you? Our brevities have had no such
       consequence: for us, an afternoon rain,

going on nineteen years this fall, through a marriage, two children, galleries, journals,
       partners, houses, gardens, letters, travels,

doubts, betrayals, work—most of it yours. I want you to tell me what you want
       beyond all that security. The people in

Human Resources ask a hard question: "Why should we hire you?" Or Goethe:
       "If you love me, what's it to me?"

When I quoted him to one of his current scholars, to find the source, she said that Goethe
       couldn't have said it, the Great Man.

He had someone say it for him, in a fiction like this. We say, in our persons,
       "I didn't mean to hurt you,"

and it's the last thing we do. But let that pass. This weekend, why don't you come over,
       take me down, kiss my breasts.

XXIV

Why don't we become prostitutes, Lewis? I don't think that market's saturated, mature.
      We're out of work; our prospects,
as our students say, both "bite" and "suck," and the money might be good. We'd have to
      sell ourselves—not in the figurative sense
the marketeers employ, to tell us we're all in sales anyway, starting with a handshake.
      One asked what I do. "I teach."
Teaching's selling. And so it goes, regardless what you profess. Professors of the Joyous
      Science, then, University of Dating.
(In Oakland, the streetwalkers call it "dating.") Our cards could read, Director, Center
      for the Study of Pleasure.
We'll need cards—calling, credit, and business. Strike that: calling and business cards
      have been synonymous since Truman.
But calling cards might be better than cell phones (legality issues?). We could print
      on condoms, hand them out;
establish brand as dealers did and do, put a new face on the second-oldest profession
      (*meum* and *tuum* is older), whose gender lines
we'd effectively cross. But our real innovation would be an evolutionary paradigm
      (tough sell, I hear you say). Then call it
fucking, a no-nonsense approach. What's fucking for? Not to know eternity. It's a stress
      reducer. On the other hand, studies show
that a woman's orgasm prepares her uterus for sperm: it isn't a luxury after all. For us
      in our new venture, that's bank
(good news, I was about to say). We trash the romantic, rule-bound bromides
      about relationship, and get down to business.
Our slogan? Got-milk?-like—but without the feminine ending, the hostile
      interrogative: "It's nothing personal."

Or maybe, "Nothing personal, it's business." "Nothing personal, just business."

Or the reverse? Let me know.

Product we have (are); customers and locations we need. And independent contractors.

But now I'm getting ahead of myself:

first capital, then human capital. This just occurred to me: with "customer service"

all the rage, now that product and price

differences are moot—by the time you've driven to the megastore, you've o'erleaped

the horse of savings and fallen on the other side—

we stand to eat the market's lunch: our service is proverb with service; so much so,

that all the pleasure we'd take

in writing copy—*Clouds in your coffee? Try our half & half*—we could easily save

the expense of. You see why:

there isn't one profitable industry out there that isn't already buying more ads for us

than we could ever track.

Talk about buy-in. Sell itself? Pay for and buy itself too.

XXV

Sadness arouses me, Mark—common enough. But it goes beyond cupidity,

      if anything goes beyond cupidity.

In love, there is no beyond. It's all here, on this body I can show you, and there, on her

      body, or his. Nor can I see how, except

in writing, that haunch I want to put my hand on, that clavicle I've rested in,

      that abdomen—how any of that is beyond me.

I, too, exfoliate from an intact (though often sounded) place, and no touch that I make

      penetrates the only integrity I know.

Tonight, at the exhibition, a painter displayed her "Two Harpies": they converse over

      the meal they've made of a man.

A textile artist, Janine I think her name was, hadn't been able to put her finger on

      the morbidity she sensed there.

I set her straight, praising as I did her long auburn hair. She moved off. Mark, they're all

      moving off: the morbid thing is here,

immanent, and I detect in myself the tiger you were always urging me to set loose.

      I wanted to praise her pants

(one of our ugliest words); and then, when she was halfway across the room, where

      hammered steel heads of mules, dogs, and boars

were meant to call us to ourselves, I thought of saying, "You might be able to sell

      a truckload of those pants, but you could sell

a harbor-full of your hair." Absurd. But the scissors snipped in my mind, and I said,

      "How dare you think I wanted anything but your pants and hair!"

XXVI

Often the hair alone will do it, especially from behind. Black, brown, blonde, red,
        magenta, blue, orange—shoulder-length
or longer. The back of a head of hair can be deceiving as the front, of course,
        but beautiful free or tied hair helps a face.
I define beauty: *symmetry barely slighted.* A woman in Borders last night, for example:
        her face, when I got around to it,
was longer than a horse's; her mouth hung open. Grossly slighted; and yet, by virtue of
        her real black hair (false black's drab)
I found myself echoing Jean, who finds no one ugly. Today, three blondes drinking tea
        in front of a bakery. I took a seat all but at their table,
the plate glass between us. I had coffee, opened *The Prime of Miss Jean Brodie*, one eye
        on the page. Magnificent teeth
of the oldest one, skin of another, smile of the third. You should have seen how self-
        sufficient they were, Lewis, how much
they enjoyed each other's presence. I stared as if to find out why, what their reasons
        were, how their stories went. The one
with the finest skin had a pin above her right brow that caught the light, the blood
        long gone. She touched it: on her bicep,
an ampersand. What for, if not to take the eye? None had wedding rings; the smile,
        the handsomest hands, wore a thick silver
band on her middle finger, the fuck-you finger, adorned like a bull's nose, like a cock
        ringed with leather, a fisted falcon's hood.
Men are nothing but balls in a sack. Snap snap: the women were gone
        when I woke from my nap.

XXVII

Would you love me, Deborah, if I wore parkas in the heat, cut my hair against my crown
        and part, drove my pants' waist halfway

down my ass, out-sized my suit—thread-bare sharkskin, color of paste—by two or three,
        wore shoes that weren't cool

when Eisenhower was, hidden in cuffs that dragged along the floor? Would you, if my art
        collapsed the spectrum into gray,

and I shaved you a soul-patch for your bikini? I could wear a thrift-store fedora, cocked
        to front my bangs, and any stove-pipe

slacks I find, Deborah, you could wear, with a blouse of chartreuse rayon. We'd make
        the most awesome pair:

my tongue studded, your right nipple pierced, each with barbed-wire tats, mine on bicep,
        yours just north of hip. Nothing would be

neat or combed or trim; there'd be no sweet disorder, no wild civility, just a garbage
        urban smash-mouth style of rude irreconcilability.

XXVIII

Hap for luck, you say, Sophia, for chance, happiness; *hab* for possession—*burg*,
>   for the place where we have them all—
the sinister, the unclear, the powerful and the plain. That's what you and I want.
>   Enough exposition already! Let's have
what's stronger and more real. Intimacy is, you say. But shyness is its fuss
>   and fear—the sober touch, the windows
open, the mid-day mad-dog deviltry that the poet need not think so. Such is our
>   profession: the splendid rat-rhyming anger
that burst upon us first when we cried before we hurt, then hurt too much to cry,
>   and then, in breathtaking suctions,
let Word dominate, struck with all our plexus hurling three feet round on any side.
>   God's as great a bore as the French
when they say He's brilliant fire, a flaming bore, a suck-hole I serve up my big
>   first serve. That ace fetters me
for the next point, makes me partial to energy, rebellion, rut—and I fall to the net
>   in toil and double, lose love-love
in straights, obey—am of rigor without pleasure. But we're always more faithful
>   than we intended to be, like Tom
through his sister to his father in *The Glass Menagerie*. My own faith's a second effort,
>   a single subjunctive I manage to lift
against what wants rest in indication—that mood. I'm angry with you because you're
>   shy, contented; you say, *"plaisir d'amour*
ne dure qu'un moment," as if it were true only of love, and not of art, business, war—
>   all of which last too long,
roughen where they rub, change old for new, give a coasting welcome to every ticklish
>   traveler, then grasp in the next

like the consummate host whose greeting parts. And *plus ça change, chagrin.*

My curse on that! Nothing lasts,

is long or hard: rough, then, very rough, be the manners of the bard.

XXIX

Amy, I got your moving letter of a month ago, while I was stationary. What's opposite
of alone? Surrounded? Smothered?

Tonight, let me be your opposite, quieter with each hour, softer, darker: just so. I have
the city to myself, and my own

worst enemy. Between us land lies, not water; still, like fish in poetry and proverb,
I'm soundless too (except here),

and fit for anything we might want to do. But it's your turn now to read, and I write
no children's book.

Do some of the things you paint make sense (I don't mean common)—to you? Some
I write make sense to me,

or the sounds of it. Others don't, I'm afraid to say: those make me against my will
avouch: "I'll quit, take up what can't fail."

Nothing there. So here I am again, standing at my station. Yours too, with its "endless
interruption and distraction"—as if a body

could maintain itself, or a mind expatiate, or a soul monadize, in any other order.
Life isn't worth the taking, Emerson said,

to do tricks in. But what I wanted to say was—I long to see you, your belongings
and your empty bowl. Maybe I have things

to put in it, mine as yours: "dreams, inhibitions, fears, fantasies, mistakes, neuroses."
Ad omnium. The listing, the sorting, never

ceases; it's the sorting out, the being sorted out, that hurts. And helps, in time. I like
the place of your responsibilities,

your "green hills and deep gardens"—their in-less, on-less, over-less, near-less-ness—
under your bed's lickerish shade.

Heartland, my Iowa, my Amy, I come to Denver in twelve days. I'll hold your palette
while you paint. I'll affect and interrupt you,

model hand, foot, shoulder, face. I'll put coffee in your cup and dinner on your plate.

I have three days. Answer me, *s'il vous plait*.

XXX

Your lover's mad again, "a bit nuts" again, almost locked up again. You skipped
       those clarities, Mark—except to say
she called the police on you, saying you were beating her (again). Yet you save her,
       kicking and screaming again, from lock-up (again),
to tell this selfless story: "She's newly struggling and trying to get a grip." Why not
       struggling, as of old, to get out of your grip,
out of the "cute apartment" you can't afford, out of the "nice new clinic to visit
       twice a week," out of "the lifetime scrip
of free Prozac"? She's twenty-one, Mark. Were there no other afflictions, she has youth.
       Let her go, not to a hospital or an institution,
but home. Don't seduce yourself by saying "We're back on track." What track? Another
       eruption of violent behavior? You flatter
yourself, my hero. Read yourself again and see. And spare me: if you hadn't hoped to
       hear my chorus, you wouldn't have
riddled me this last catastrophe you engineered: instead of staying at home
       to watch TV with Laura (her plan, however modest),
you dragged her into yours: seizing a ballroom flush with money and women,
       open bar, ample food, fine wine—
and all for the cause of art, your cause. Laura, in her tight black shift, was an ornament,
       a Cressid, *a daughter of the game.*
You think she missed *your roving eye, your gift for the runaround?*
       (Not after four years, if it took her a day.)
I witnessed the scene she made, smoking on the escalator, while you, at the first table,
       traced your descent from Cartier-Bresson
and John Cage, improvising a malapropism for the patrons that was spontaneous
       twenty years ago, when you spoke it

on the water tower (of a squirrel that leapt, and, to our tripping amazement, lived),

        and I relished it in a poem.

But not that night, as the gist of your aesthetic: "We're instamatic." Always

        protagonist of happenstance, Mark,

and innocent of consequence (Laura's eruption, in this case). I see our quality

        in the Greeks—Achilles, Odysseus, Clytemnestra,

Philoctetes . . . the list goes on and on: past masters all of the "passive-aggressive" *ethos*.

        That we exist may be

the gross of the problem; if so, I'll take it one peck at a time. What does the hero's

        insistence on his own way get him?

Laura likes her own recipe, too: add injury to insult. Don't queer the dish with ingredients

        you never use. Or take it this way:

you're more than twice her age. Call me if you need anything. I'm alone.

XXXI

As I was about to propose a shift in our thinking about prostitution, your letter arrived.

       "You need to get out more: women don't have to

pay for it (oh, they pay, but from a store of value, not in a medium of exchange).

       The market whose lunch you say we'll eat

never existed. Nor have you even begun to think through what, if it did, that market

       would look like. Ever been to the mall?

Imagine all those pork-bellied men were women, and the women too. There's your

       clientele. But it's your premise I object

to: you and I are already independent contractors (with good benefits). Why launch

       a venture bound to leave us where we started?

As for your tacit assumption that your scheme would incur no overhead. Ridiculous.

       Shakespeare had overhead; and as Iago

is nothing if not critical, business is nothing if not overhead—especially now, when even

       a word like *threepeat* can be monetized.

They'd license our breath to us if they could. Stop reading *Business Week*."

       Fair enough, Lewis, but too late; I was reading

something in it just the other day, without being sure I was getting the tone right

       (a problem you seem to have had

with me): a man's—maybe a stand-up comedian's—account of his start-up.

       He'd offer women his *ear*.

That, it seemed to him, after market research and his own "listening experience, over

       four decades," was the organ women

really desired in men. So I devised a simple experiment that afternoon, to see if I could

       duplicate his results. I quote:

"I can get laid any night of the week," Jill said, "but that's not what I want." She paused.

       "Are you still there? Are you still

coming for dinner?" Dutifully, I asked if I might bring anything. "It's already attached."

   I could hear the armor in her humor

clank. Jokes—the bloodless violence of everyday life. I'd touched a discussion I didn't

   want to have, whose theme is, what?—

those *lineaments of gratified desire* Blake required (after fighting with his wife).

   Jill and I have no love to renew

by falling out; we're not faithful friends; she knows it, I know it. At best, we're brave

   strangers. But to get back to

entrepreneurship, for the impecunious, the—(I lost the word; looking into the Random

   House College, "predacious" I found):

paid listeners are plentiful, aren't they? This man, this stand-up or staff writer,

   couldn't have been serious.

Therapists—years ago, I thought I might make a good therapist, if I could be a Freudian,

   but that's an overdetermined market,

and anyway Oprah's cornered it. Talking never cured anything (yours excepted:

   I leave whoring to men).

You must have had a few of those conversations that, designed to bring a relationship

   full-circle, end up carrying it on:

where you'd meant to be at home reading Kenneth Boulding by eight, you fucked

   and spent the night instead. I know I have;

the ear is love's second port, no matter which Neo-Platonist you read. Talk's erotic:

   even men without a woman's touch know that.

The other night, after dinner, Jill offered me "a gigolo fee" after dessert; I spent the night.

   I have been faithful, Lewis, *in my fashion,*

these thirty years, and see nothing but contract labor from here on out. ("Penurious":

   there's the word I wanted above. I'll be that too.)

XXXII

"That was a thoughty question," said General Myers, in Baghdad, with a laugh,

   "just the kind we like at meetings

of the Joint Chiefs," of which he's chief. For chiefs, thought's definitely a dual-use item.

   Which is fine: nothing is but what

our purposes for it are: boots on the ground, in this case, the ground being sandy.

   Hard to get traction there; a place

you could really get out the ass in, if you're not careful. Better, though, to be forward-

   leaning than risk-averse. The latter's

what got us into this quagmire in the first place. We need to full-scrub those old plans

   and then clean-sheet it. You can't soft on these killers;

you have to hard over on them, be robust. Mark, I hope this is more than another confab

   on the margins, to speak in Scooter Libby,

but I doubt it. Our interest in and objection to the language leaders speak will amount

   to nothing. You and I aren't force multipliers;

we're unpatriotic, idiotic members of elites: our lines of operation (*passim*) cross

   on no graph with no slices of regime power;

like Clinton and his administration, we embody reflexive pullback; our guidance

   is all wrong, *sans* shock, *sans* awe.

We have no tradecraft or relevant HUMINT; even our body language, suboptimized,

   idles, diddles: this is a plastic, teachable

moment, and we're not grinding away on it, war-gaming it out: we play small ball.

XXXIII

You've become a consultant, Lewis? Scholarship wasn't good enough? You had law,

       medicine; you could have been a rabbi—

and now you consult? *Caveat vendor*, then, because that's what you are.

       I was consulted to just the other day,

in the temp office I was temping in—and I almost bought in. He was seeing the whole

       picture, not just rattling off arbitrary solutions;

trying to get his mind around it—when the co-CEO called a halt. *They fucked me*, he said.

       Sympathetic, I stopped him on his way out,

offered to walk him to his car. Within three hundred yards, he'd recapped his spiel.

       But this time, his *ethos* was false;

so, too, his *pathos* and his *logos*. I liked him. "We've got this syringe, and we're injecting

       a little light into your window, to frame the game.

You know, we don't sell cars here, we sell mobility systems. And who wants to sign off

       on that? It could be sayonara.

Where're they gonna stand if you're standing on their leverage point? They're not gonna

       sign off on that. You're stepping on your dick.

You can't just airdrop your intellectual capital on their hot zone. They wanna know

       if you're going to the mountaintop with them.

If you think you're there already, they don't need you. They want some action, not some

       literature. They don't wanna be confused

at a higher level, thank you very much. You can talk until you're blue in the face

       about solutions multipliers. You have rhetoric,

you have content, you have process, you have clientele—but where does that get you

       at the end of the day? Your handles, your levers,

your trading regimes, your offsets. They don't wanna hear about it. Where's your staff?

       Who's gonna do this? Oh, you're ramping up to that,

the staff's ramping up. But the clock's ticking and their burn-rate's ramping up.

       That's their time and money you're talking about.

Well, I've got two things to say about money and time: nobody has any and everybody

       has a shitload. Lemme just let you in

on that little secret. It comes down to what people want. And you know what that is?

       It's A to Z, and fast. It's a cab to Mars.

If we don't do something today about Mars, we're gonna regret it tomorrow,

       so you'd better put your best

mobility profiler on it day before yesterday. Maybe there isn't any water on Mars.

       They don't wanna hear it.

You get some water there, because the wars are gonna be fought over water. Mars

       has canals, they say. Well so the fuck does Venice,

and look at the Venetians. They're drowning, sinking, getting muddy. The whole world

       is mud. But you keep your mouth shut.

How out in front of it can you be? That's the real question. You can forget your conflict

       avoidance and your business models.

That's all academic. This is real-world we're talking, boots on the ground. Economies

       of scale, profit centers, competitive advantage—

don't waste my time. Save the lecture. Greenfields, brownfields, daylighting, sprawl,

       quality of life—those topics are a little too

20th-century. They know everything's a catalyst for everything else. They know

       your vision-across-boundaries, your

whole-systems thinking. They're tired of hearing that every condition pre-exists

       somewhere. That's for you to get your arms around.

Capture it, leverage it, fuck it. And fuck full sentences, too. Curtailment or efficiency?

       That's the question. And the bottom line?

People don't wanna be curtailed or efficient. And they don't wanna know it all—

the stranded costs, the hidden costs, the cost barriers.

It is all they want to know. Of course, you're not trying to sell corporations a spending

program. You're selling a frame.

Just put it out there. They'll play. You give them the language, they'll sign off.

The umbrella solution. The over-bridging

under-girding all-embracing solution. Well, lemme tell you: they won't sign off.

They don't want you telling them what to do.

They want you telling them how to do what they wanna do. That's what consultants

are for. And if you can't do it, they'll call in the lawyers."

I liked him, as I said, though I wouldn't want to be his "inside champion." And without

one of those, tunneling under the dead-enders

to form a virtual network, you'll never reach the tipping point, achieve first-user

advantage, leapfrog the competition, piggyback

the old guard, and then spin off a half dozen game-changing ventures. Just now,

writing these words, I think of my consultant

as Thomas Sheridan thought of Swift: so entirely loyal to truth and plain dealing that,

in all affairs of the world, if not even

in the solitude of his study, he was "a hypocrite in reverse." So far has satire fallen,

Lewis, that I confuse Swift's savage indignation

with my consultant's sour grapes. But is there another literary kind consulting compares

more favorably with? Another career path

that pays as handsomely for "the exposure and correction of vice"? Not to mention

one that spares you carrying overhead (by the way,

I'm stealing your identification of business and Iago for a user's manual on

"visionary leadership")—as no doubt you've

bounded from contract labor to full-time employment. Congratulations are in order

     (let's have dinner next week).

In closing, let me say that even though I find this scheme of yours "all one"

     with mine, I hope consulting

provides you with better pay and benefits than whoring.

XXXIV

"Success is counted sweetest"—you were coming today, Paula; in my dream last night,
     all was arrival, bed: there we were,
after thirty years: you upset, I hungry. Not quite perfection, but (including Emily's lines),
     all in motion. All. That word again, the marker
of constitutions, not of fats or lotteries. "Success is counted sweetest"—I had to piss;
     that's what set it off. Usually three times before I
fall off, reading, after midnight, I have to get up and go. Something, I was told, with the
     prostate; something about that gland losing
elasticity. And there's the flavored seltzer I drink between ten and two. Anyway, in this
     order of things, in real time, as they say,
where separation and independence rule, you were coming to Denver today, on business.
     Were: the action of fitting failed.
And I'd known it had, known you weren't coming today, for seven days. "I'm afraid,"
     you began, "I'm not coming next week
as planned." Every meeting you'd "lined up" but one "fell apart." Was I that one,
     half of it? You'd never think of me
as a lined-up meeting, would you? But we had planned, in effect, a businessless meeting.
     Last night, reading David Bohm's
On Creativity ("the implicate order"), I didn't understand, until after shutting the book,
     how fitting all his words I'd copied were,
had been, would be, are—each and all at once, in "mutually dependent origination." All
     that's lined up falls apart; all can be
rescheduled for July, as you say your trip can. We'll have to see, won't we. Which
     particular July, in this explicate order we find ourselves
in, happens to be "one year since I saw you last." To consciousness—or, as my students
     and our president say, "conscious"—years

are as seconds, if so much, and those, partial orders like dreams, such as the one I had of
       you last night. We were in bed, making love;
we were unclothed, for the most part (skin just gets in the way), and headlong, hungry.
       I wanted to retard myself but couldn't.
You were upset—as, on like occasions in our past, you had been. I worried my pre-
       maturity, you, your worry. We sighed, we grunted.
You got up, went to the bathroom; into the bed, taking your place, came Katie, to
       "encourage" me, she said. Imagine! Already leaking,
if not spermed out (if "timed out" and "bled out," why not? What are we but blood and
       time?), I hardly needed a surrogate for you,
even if I'd always lusted after Katie. Out of what order came she? Gone as soon as there,
       only to be replaced—but not in bed—
by your roommate, a man in your room (your husband?). It was the first of June; he
       made you out a check for the month's rent,
by which time you were back in bed. I know, because he said he wanted to see which one
       of us had "pants" on. Had I been panting?
You dismissed him. "Success is counted sweetest": I had to piss, and knew that if I got up
       then to go, my performance would improve.
(Listen to me: is that the way my conscious talks?) *Coitus interruptus* knew no bounds,
       but the dream knew its Freud, had been read into
him. In life as in the dream I had to piss: piss is water, water is life, *la vida es sueño.*
       Enfoldment, as Bohm defines it, is "a movement in which
everything, any particular element of space, may have a field which unfolds into the
       whole and the whole enfolds it in it."
I fell asleep admiring that *it in it*, wanting a like ending to come out of me. A week ago,
       you were "feeling a bit mixed-up."

I wanted to answer you in "a language . . . of similar differences and different

  similarities"; to describe, as you did, what feeling

mixed-up feels like. But men don't speak, as a rule, about feeling mixed-up, unless that's

  like shit or *okay*. And when did

"mixed-up" become a feeling? And how to describe each *mixed*, each *up*? I couldn't

  answer you immediately. When I could, I couldn't send:

my ISP and SMPT lacked "suitable similarities," and so formed a wall instead of a pipe, a

  clash of partial orders, each well defined, but together

"functionally wrong." Most men are. I had to piss; my dream of you enfolded that, to

  hold me there, protect my sleep. Protect itself,

too, from what Bohm calls "a deeper and more extensive inner movement" that

  "ultimately dissolves structure." Urine is structure

dissolved. And the thinking of the body, which gets us into bed at all, overcame it all—

  Freud's idea of the dream, the dream, you within—

and moved me to the bathroom, just as you were coming out. You'd had to go, I had to

  go—this inter-auto suggestiveness

out of which even logic comes. "Movement gives shape to all forms; Structure gives

  order to movement; Movement dissolves structure."

QED, Bohm. Your thought of seeing me scares you "a little," yet you're "sad not to

  at the same time. But now that I think about it,

that's how I've often felt in anticipation of seeing you/not seeing you." A week ago I

  couldn't, and today again can't, say the same thing.

Success is counted sweetest, I woke up saying, instantly sad to slip from that highway

  into the high prairie of the day.

Hard cock in hand, I went to piss. Men can't (can any animal?) piss and come at once.

  Badly I needed to do the one

and wanted to do the other. Aroused and having to go—the human condition. You, too,

  fretted your performance; both of us

sought a high order of satisfaction—the action, "the movement of fitting." We wanted

  the science and the art

articulate, to *surrey on down to a stoned soul picnic*. I softened, standing over the bowl,

  and went; then, taking a dab of lotion

in my left hand, went back to bed to find you, knowing better. Not a clue. Instead, this—

  and my slightly stiff dick,

and dawn, birdsong, dogbark, my brother making breakfast. As I wrote, the lotion

  thinned. It dried up in the friction.

I spit on myself, trying to and not to, put you, keep you, in my mind's eye. Others flitted

  past and in, and nothing came.

I reached for the K-Y, as one might try for objectivity, when your Lemon Up, loosed

  from history, drew in, its scent nearly full

on your red hair, above and below, and our mouths on each other, knowing more love

  than they could ever know,

the new subdivision hillside tilting us up, our volumes to show . . . then New Year's Eve,

  twenty years later, enthralled at the foot

of Pam and Susan's stairs, my right hand on your underpants. "No," you said, "I can't,

  I can't." That was your fiancé,

then implicate groom, husband and roommate now. The neutral jelly turned desiccant.

  Success is counted sweetest

By those who ne'er succeed. To comprehend a nectar Requires sorest need. And even so

  I came; what man, undamaged, can't?

Still, my bedroom occupation. "I want to hear your voice," you ended your note.

  I want to hear your voice.